Red Hot
on a
Silver Note

by
Maketa Groves

CURBSTONE PRESS

Printed in Canada on acid-free paper by Best Book Manufacturers
Cover design: Chris Thorkelson

This book was published with the support of the
Connecticut Commission on the Arts and the National
Endowment for the Arts.

Library of Congress Cataloging-in-Publication Data

Groves, Maketa.
       Red hot on a silver note / by Maketa Groves. — 1st ed.
       p.   cm.
       ISBN 1-880684-22-5
       1. Title.
     PS3557.R747R43
     811'.54—dc20   96-869

published by
CURBSTONE PRESS   321 Jackson Street   Willimantic, CT 06226
    phone: (860) 423-5110   e-mail: curbston@connix.com
              http://www.connix.com/~curbston/

Acknowledgments

Several of these poems have been previously published by the following: *Image and Imagination, Lotus Press, Morena Magazine, Poetry USA,* and *Spoken Word Press.*

I would like to thank Margot Pepper, Ben Clark, and Kathy and Arthur Horn for their support and encouragement in the making of this book. I would also like to thank Jack Hirschman and Sarah Menefee for their friendship, faith in this project, and unwavering support through the years. Much love to all who read this work.

This book is dedicated to the memory of my father, Levi C. Smith, who named me, taught me my first poem, and turned me loose in the world, to love.

CONTENTS

Red Hot on a Silver Note

Do We All Have These Images?

Do we all have these images
of our mothers
down on their knees
scrubbing the kitchen floor
after midnight
while we went to bed
long ago
but just
got up for a drink of water
or a trip
to the bathroom
and saw this image
of our mother?

Do we all have these images
of tiny women
or raw-boned
on their knees
scrubbing
sponges
rags
moving over the floor
slowly
as they
work out their
problems
alone,
and deep within
themselves
sending

unwelcome
energy
into their sponges
as if cleaning
the floor would
make the world
right
like bills getting
paid
and troublesome things
people said
vanishing
from their thoughts
like rain?

Do we all have these images
of our mothers
bent over kitchen floors
kitchen sinks
their hands deep
in dish water
as though some invisible
being
held their hands
and promised them
wonderful things
husbands and children
could not?

Do we all have these images
of our mothers
heads on their arms
in exhaustion
they share with walls
and floors and sinks
because husbands and
children are sleeping
and only now are they
free to be exhausted?

Do we all have these images
of our mothers
tiny women
or raw-boned
moving across kitchen floors
hands buried deep in apron
pockets
or laughing
like little girls
their child-woman
moving through them
like a breeze
rippling emotions
in their faces
like ripe wheat
in a gentle wind?

Do we all have these images
of mothers:
their bowed backs
their buried girls
emerging
from time to time
their hands
moving slowly
across floors
of linoleum
like linoleum
was a prayer?

Family History

We sprang from the verdant fields
of the Mississipi Delta
strong young limbs moving
among grass and wheat
as though
native to its bloodshed

I exist in this place where stars fall
through ceilings
and fathers
teach
their daughters
the language of Poe

My father exalting
. . . "the Raven, nevermore"
fell so icy,
grotesque
from the lips
of an eight year old

I exist in a place
deep
dank
still
as still as the
Delta swamps
at midday
as still as
the butterfly

drinking
sticky
sweet nectar.

I exist where
the heart was cut out
ripped across
miles of regret
and anger
as lushness
fell to metal
as Africa became
Mississippi
as Mississippi
became Michigan
the new land.

I exist in the place
where carved and looming
furniture was dusted
every day without fail
young hands
stroking polished wood
bundles of food
taken to the neighbor woman
who screamed
her collective remembrances
of Voodoo Gods
who came

to get her
give her elixirs
drop fruits into
goblets of blood:
her collective memories
of circle dances
and female rites of passage.

I exist in this place!
Here, I mix MY elixers
practice human sacrifices
take ancient red clay
throw its dust
upon the floor
create gris gris
pray for the souls
of zombies
sleep with orchids
fastened to my eyelids

I exist in this place
I exist in this place
I exist in this place
even now
as I speak.

Bathed in Raptures

Bathed in raptures
of Poe
from an early age—
my father and I studying Poe's sad
and frightened voice
my father's face a study in delight
in Poe's awareness of
the power of darkness
I have toiled alongside Poe
in the urban ghettos—
dug in deep in Detroit
New York
New Orleans
and San Francisco.

Poe
everyone speaks of his madness
his exquisite madness
which drove him
loving his blood relation
drinking in Baltimore ghetto pubs,
eventually the gutters

what unparalleled madness!
what kindred spirits of insanity to embrace!
what cataclysmic inner eruptions
to experience!!

How could I be other than
an urban mad wild woman
bathed in the raptures
of your strange plot twists,
and stranger characters?

Art is an abyss
we choose to enter
or avoid.
But, Poe,
you chose me—
your twisted fingers
and blackened mouth
pointing the way
towards endless raptures—
I enter!
 I enter!

North End Girls (For Carmen)

In the summer of '72, Fats Dominoe
(no relation to the singer),
went in for hiring "girls"
to pump gas
in his
East Detroit
service station.

Best girl friend
heard about it
and enlisted me
to flush out the scam
thinking no gas fumes
could match
my fire-brand
noxious ways.

Me and Carmen
went enrolled
to pump gas,
and wound up pumping up hearts
at the same time
trying not to settle
for what
our mothers
"had to"
we floundered
young
and awkward
in womanflesh.

Pumping gas
in bell-bottomed jeans
flowered short sleeved blouses
in summertime
wild daisies
tall sunflowers
spilling yellow
across
customer tire threads
we were careful
not to hold
a gaze
too long
we were novel
we were famous
"GIRLS AT THE PUMP!"

Careful
to hide our
young hearts
from the many ways
to get into trouble,
we wed ourselves to the service station.

In the summer of '72, Fats Dominoe
hired two girls from the North End
to tend his East Detroit
service station,
left them to close

hot summer nights
left them branded "handlers"
because they were
from the inner-city.

In twenty years
only four other
female gas station
attendants
have I seen;
maybe the idea is too suggestive:
young women
intimate
interiors of cars
soft breasts
brushing chrome and steel. . .

but,
in the summer
of '72
Fats Dominoe
hired college "girls"
from the North End.

Detroit

city of cars
city of churches
city by lakes
city of trees
city of internal conflict
city of tears
city of sudden violence
city of Marxist predictions
come true
this is for you!

city of good friends:
lynn
savva
diane
ernesto
judy
greg, and all the harrises
patty cohen
the three leos
enos
gary and ruth
who held
up in my quarters all night
scratching
cursing
for not being able
to love
because of
the junk

coursing through
their veins
and me
cursing them
for lack of sleep
and wondering
why
the 'burbs'
also
produced junkies
and whores
and why
the whole world
was such a
messed-up place
seen from
my eyes that night

This is to Steven
who with
flashing black
Yugoslavian eyes
 bashed pigs' heads
in the slaughterhouses
of Detroit
while crying
about the contradictions
of America

DETROIT
city of unexpected delights
like being thirteen
years old
and invited
down the street
to listen
to the
"legendary blues great"
play his guitar
at a home barbecue
though
he was no legend then
but one of us

City of the first freeway
to carry
the instruments
of war
to the front
where is your peace?

city of factories
that controlled our lives
and seduced our will
and
broke the backs of the old men
and the spirits
of the young
our

every moment
was dedicated
to you
so
in a smoldering summer night
Leo #1 and Duane
shot the neon lights
of your
flashing "FORD HAS A BETTER IDEA"
out
into what we thought
would be a better day.

city of creators
city of inventors
of innovators
city of the finest spirits
and
greatest contradictions.

city of the gurus
of cass corridor
who mesmerized
the summer of '70
in a frenzied madness
and
culminated in the cries
of "BROTHERS", and embrace
to the cops
who came to haul

us off to jail
for having a
bare ass mescaline romp
under the stars
of Belle Isle summer night
and
leo #3 cried,
"maketa, roll a joint
on the left side
of the bullhorn"
and I did
and those cops turned
the radio
to the local jazz station
and became quite mellow
which goes to show
kindness sometimes comes
in the strangest ways
love is all powerful
we are all one
DETROIT
RISE
and SHINE!

To A Homeless Woman Knitting

How can you sit there
working your fingers so
in the dark corner of the courtyard
your back bowed against the urge to
not attempt some sane and normal
activity
your back bowed in resistance to
the streets that would claim you?
claim your broken fingers
your fat mouth
your little old lady hair bun
your eyes
your toes
your furrowed brow
your plaid coat

your tongue
that
whips around your
lips as you attempt
a difficult loop

You should be in some
living room where pictures
of your children
or your sister's children
or your brother's children
line your walls
and doilies lie
on backs of overstuffed

and musty chairs
and you should watch the
morning news as you knit—
your cup of tea or coffee
beside you
your feet up
on some foot stool
that was bought especially
for you
years ago when people
cared to do such things
for little old ladies

But no, here you sit!
your presence overwhelming
me
that I should walk past
you to my office
you old enough to
be my mother
or my grandmother
that you do not have
a place to sit
that is more comfortable
than a concrete step!

I am ashamed for you!
I am ashamed for me!
and this society
that claims civilization

but cannot place an
old woman in decent housing!

I don't think it's because
they think
you're crazy,
and I don't think you're crazy
and they have no right to question
your sanity
and I need to know why they
have done this to you!

At Saint Anthony's

I almost ran up to her to say,
"Hey Jazzy, you coming to workshop, today"?
but saw her head
turned towards the wall
of St. Anthony's
like a broken doll's head
and her exhausted hungry eyes;
and I remembered:
being poor
takes twice
the effort.

Master of the Blue Note
(Mantra for Miles Dewey Davis)

CHOP
ZHOP
ZWE-BOP

Oh my soul!
Oh my soul!
Oh my soul!

Light years!
Miles years!
feather drop light
hammer drop hard
Light years!
a step
a light
swirling
around you
dropcloth of garments
so much color
and light
mixtures
juxtapositions
Light years

Oh my soul!
Oh my soul!
Oh my soul!

Eye dance
trance envelop me
in your stare
glare
hypnotic eye
dance!

Spill me
through
note after note
until I am saturated
and drawn thin
cool and satisfied
as your rhythms

Spring step
half step
No!
never you
always
the full step
to your own drummer
praying and pounding
inside your head

Oh my soul!
Oh my soul!
Oh my soul!

Given to us
like a present
to shine
you burned
down to cinders
encapsulating
the flames
in space
enough to
burn bright,
brighter
broken down
to
RED HOT
ON A SILVER NOTE

. . . we hung onto
binding that note
to us like a love
entwining
ourselves
in it's charms,
pulled and
rung out
in subtle embrace.

Oh my soul!
Oh my soul!
Oh my soul!

Leapt
wept
pulled
back
from your stare
affixed to
the pinpoint
of your
eyebeams
straight
steady
eyebeams

Wrung out
spun out:
your blue
notes pulled us
turned us
into ourselves
to examine
in purity
scorched
in soul
burned through
paper thin
turned out
and back again

Oh my soul!
Oh my soul!
Oh my soul!

CHOP
ZHOP
ZWE-BOP

How you lived!
How you played!
Hard
thin ridge
of bone
around
delicate frame
of steel will
doctor's son
unhumbled one!

Master of the blue note,
elfin, wafer
thin love
waif:

You were no
"prince of darkness",
BUT pure and crystalline
LIGHT!

A Wild Woman Must Remain Wild

A wild woman must remain wild
has to move through her life
like an arrow
has to pick her friends carefully
to dance the lunata
to change her direction
if she feels the urge. . .

A wild woman must remain wild
so
the wild birds will know it's okay
to eat from her hand
their eyes wild like hers

A wild woman must remain wild
all her life
throw in some left curves
move to the mountains
pick wildflowers
inhabit a flat in Soho
paint self portraits
love the sight of little old ladies
and men sitting on city park benches

A wild woman must remain wild
send her life beams
through the energy field
of the universe
like a comet.

Jane's House

Jane's house is on sale
for half a million
dollars!

I passed it the other day
on the bus
I was just able to read
the sign
before it faded in the distance
it said:
"Historic railroad car
for sale, $500,000.

Did we ever think of it as
a railroad car?
Was it worth so much Jane
so many years ago—
those years when we were so much like
crustaceans—
hard on the outside, and
soft in the middle?

It was like our doll house then
only we were the dolls arranging and
rearranging
the furniture
changing our costumes
and

staring pensively into the
North Bay with Pinocchio eyes—

I miss Jane and her
crazy guitar. . .

Jane's house is on sale for
half a million dollars—
was it worth so much Jane,
back then
when you played your guitar
and we beat out the blues
slapping and rapping
on spoons
and tabletops
dipping and diving—
two girls a little frightened
but bouncing music off
the walls?

Where I'm From

Where I'm from
     Things don't flow like they used to
     like when we wuz little
and
     water flowed from city hydrants
down
     our faces in the summer time
and wuz
     sweeter than kool-aid
and
     mineral smell popped
up out of the earth to find
the very best olfactory nerves

I MEAN WE COULD SMELL
THE EARTH!

Cumulus clouds ranged the sky
     thunderstorms tore down the
atmosphere
     sent us shivering
     running
     to hide under our beds
as lightning shrieked and
DANCED!

BACKWOODS and URBAN
met and tangled
and came up with a new

thang in human—
      with the gait of a cat
      the mouth of a split-melon
AND THE HEART OF A GARGOYLE!

Where I'm From

      music never was the tune
      but IS the language
      stolen from the lips
      as soon as it
      hit cold air
to become a wail, a cry
      a blues born of driving pistons,
and
      steel
      cylindrical buildings
      mounting and humping
      on the sky!

AND LOVE ran deep—

      an ancient plume of water starting
high
      up in the Appalachians
      running down, down towards the

MISSISSIPPI
      through bends of minuscule
contortions
      through fine, jagged, ragged rock
      twisting and turning
back over itself
      so frail and narrow in places
IT'S PLAIN WORN OUT
and won't go no more
but
      is there anyway
and
      runs and flows and mixes finally
quiet and deep
      in a valley stream..

AND
      summers were so hot
      they melted you from the inside out
      and days didn't cool down
until midnight
when
      crickets came to join you
      in minuets
and
      homage to the moon.

WHERE I'M FROM . . .

MEN BE SO COOOOLLL . . .
they walk
and you think
they DANCE!

Yosemite Series

I. (Fantasy)

After darkness
I steal out
to tempt
the brown bear:
bits of meat
clutched in
my trembling hand
I wish to see
its magnificent face
to feel its claw
rip the food
from my grasp
perhaps
re-arrange my anatomy
in the process
my well preserved
anatomy
(for someone my age)

But it doesn't come
this brown bear
it doesn't rip me
or maim me
it leaves me to ponder
once again
there is little

we can do
to change
the natural order
of things.

II. Half Dome

Walking towards your many faces
I cannot say who moves:
you or I
pressed against the sky
you draw me
granite black and green.
You are the colors
everything else becomes.

III.

Oh great rock anointed with
blood of pine
oil
brown nettle forest bed
You have captured my heart!
rendered me under your spell
given me your secrets
and

I am woven into
your fabric
your nature cloth
of forest green
and granite rock
wood of bark
and
blue of sky
weave me more
until
I blend
perfect and still:
a dark brown stitch.

IV.

Why are they attracted
by the noise?
these humans who sit
where the
water rushes over rocks?

I prefer the stillness
of the forest
broken only
by the chirping of winged birds
and
the sounds of trees

whispering
into the silent wind.

V.

Slate
gray
granite face
cooled by
the autumn breezes
enchanting
you loom above me
like a lover
If I may make
such a shameless and Freudian
comparison

You are so precise
in your coolness:
(I have always preferred
preciseness in lovers,
and coolness, too).

VI.

What is more lovely
than
your red bark
your grey squirrels?
your bears
who never show
themselves
but growl softly
into the velvet
of your starry nights?

Fisherman

On smoothly
worn rocks

at the edge. . .
of the western world
he stands.

Two lines
cast deep
into the sea
hunched against
cold and wind,
he resembles
something inanimate:
beached seaweed,
a still-life
of patience.

The sky
rains down
no sudden moves
are made here,
knowing the rock
the winds
the rains
sea foam
spews
against
his refuge,
waves spill

and pour
upon him.

Eyes cast
deep
into the sea
he sees no
more than
you or I
but,
looks
longer
deeper

perhaps
he has
secrets
with the fish
divines wisdom
from the
tide pools
speaks
to the whales
plunges
to their
depths
plays/rampages
on the sea bottom.

Wild and crazy
on the beach
I stand
whipped by wind
filled with excitement
at the edge of the
western world

What knowledge
is culminated
at these last shores?

I want to go there
to stand above
the pounding surf
to taste
the salt crystals.

I want to go
to the melancholy
and lonely rock
touched
only by indifferent waves
and patient feet.

Reflections on turning 43

When I was young,
it was a bird frame
that encaged my soul
made of it
a jangled
raw
dangling nerve-ending
bird-wire thin
fragile
and flighty thing.

When I was young,
the bird thing
was strung out
on being
raw and unstable
always perched
on the edge of
its seat
waiting for flight.

But the bird thing
has metamorphosized
from its original
ectomorph frame
to somewhere
in between
say,
an ecto/endomorph,
in short,

a more massive thing
a sure footed thing

At first
I was not accepting
of this thing
crying out,
where is my bird?
where is my frightened
fragile thing
in that so, so tiny body?!

This new body thing
around my soul
demands more food
is aggressive
and sure footed
has bulk
and muscle
and moves
with more purpose

I didn't know
if I could live
with this
starting work-outs
praying to see
the bird thing

when I looked
in the mirror

no bird thing

just this massive
self assured thing
that stands
with her feet
slightly apart
well rounded
swivel hips
small firm breasts
that still have points
hard thighs
more fleshly all over
but firm and round!

I guess it's the roundness—
birds only have angles
planes
lines for definition
but this new rounded thing...

so,
I struggled with it
tried to hide the roundness
No!

I don't want to look
like a Reubens' painting
No!

Take me back
bird thing
take me back
to my original shape!

But the ecto/endo thing
prevailed

And one day
driving along
(of all times),
the rounded thing
GOT to me
I saw it
really saw it,
and said YEAH!

flesh is okay
firm flesh will do
I am a part of the
earth now!
I am solid
and I'm
strong
and I can still
work out

and have this body
this earth mother
thing
this weighted thing
that has more power
than a bird body
I don't want to fly
or die
'cause flight is
death for a human
who thinks she is
a bird!

But this
laden
with weight
and abundance thing
is so natural
and so real
and so much a part
of the eternal wheel
of life
my soul is ringing
inside
singing praises
wants no other home
than this
in the natural order
of things.

Open Letter to Tracy Chapman

Tracy—
you drove your fast car across the border
and unto the fat stage of grammy queendom

you proudly rose from your seat and
made your way towards the stage in dreadlocks
jeans
and leather jacket.
you didn't tinsel out
you didn't sing about love
as another commodity to buy and sell.

There was no sturdy male to smile
at you
to kiss you
you walked up without the fanfare
knowing
a man would have wanted you to
straighten your hair
and flutter your hands primly
like those victorian ladies whose
hands seldom had to leave their laps
except to flutter prettily.

but your hands don't flutter
they plant themselves around
your guitar
like a mother around a child
and pluck at the life chords of
songs
of countless black girls

crying soundlessly for the "fast car"
to come in the night.

Your hands moved towards the grammy
you wrought from the heartache of
American dreams moving away too fast
like your car.

Thank you for this reflection of us black girls
whose hearts desire to fly
and "be someone"
but whose voices hold the rancor of urban
blight
and too often whose only flight
is to the stoops of the tenement.

We black girls thank you
we urban ghetto angels
whose dreams flutter around
our bottled-up hearts.

and . . .
 those of you
who are listening
do not take this letter
as a sigh of self-pity
or defeat;

The fast car comes in for
one of us every day,

and every day we ride upon
the monstrous invention
the V8 pumping
the dual exhaust exhausted

Black girls are no strangers
to the smooth upholstery
the crooning radio
the ability to go
from 0 to 65 in a matter of seconds

What the HIStory books
won't tell you
is that black girls
MUST accelerate in order to survive,

and...
  WE DO!

Gina,
Evangelina,
Marilyn &
Roxanne

Elegantly plumed
    blossomed out
        as delicate desert
Yucca tree flowers,
the ladies of the Tenderloin
strut their stuff

Pendants, oversized false pearls
    zirconium diamonds
        adorn their necks
    throats
    hang
from their ears
    lobes dragged down by baubles,
orbs of glitter

All aflutter the ladies strut
their stuff
Gina,
    Evangelina,
        Marilyn &
Roxanne
along the Tenderloin streets
bauble and bead-light
    preceeding them

fine
                    imitation French perfume
waifing along the air
            whenever they can get it

These are the soft voiced ones
            the whispery ones
the rough voiced masculine ones

unafraid of the sounds
            of their own male voices
aloft on the wind
as they tottle down the sidewalk
in high heels and little dresses

Men in dresses
            entering those oddly
chartered waters
            that all society
fails to understand—

it frightens us so!

These men in dresses
            scorning their sex
                    applying make-up
with fine brush strokes
worrying about tummy tucks
and the cost of a permanent operation

transforming them from bodies
　　　　they shun to their
　　　　ultimate fantasies:
Ladies of the Tenderloin
　　　　Gina,
　　　　　　　　Evangelina,
Marilyn　&
　　　　Roxanne

Such colorful, colorful ladies!
　　　　such alive ladies
　　　　　　　who live to smile
their *ladies* smile
　　　　shop with thoughtfully
wrinkled brows
who say such things as, "oh
God, how hard I tried to be a male
　　　　child for my father!"

These ladies, these fine
　　　　specimens of boy/girls
who befriend a friend with
the passion of
thirst for water
staring out from
their desert habitats
　　　　these fine Yucca
blossoms

I would defend each one
        saying they have
a right to be here
        to be seen
                to be heard
Let the viewer turn from them
        if their eyes
                mirror too much our
skewered humanity

If their rough-edged voices
        sweet, soft titters
remind the listener of their
        own lost, forgotten,
                hidden voices
clasp your ears

I have seen their humanity
        It is immense
                enveloping
sisterly
When Gina clasps me to her
        huge bosom,
                she is celebrating life

I will not desert them
        claim I do not value
                their friendship,
their lives are on the line
        every day

I will not run from their disease of
    love
    nor judge their sexuality
    sex being such a complex
        and mystifying thing
    anyway

I will not turn my nose
    when they tell
    me they
    have been turning tricks
I will smell their fear
    their sexual conquests
    their fight for survival

I will not sacrifice one of them
    to the so-called 'Gods
    of decency'
        and
    when they tell me they
    are going—
    slipping away
        diseased
unloved
    unwanted

    In my prayers for momma, for poppa
    for brother and sister
        I will include them

Gina,
            Evangelina,
Marilyn &
    Roxanne

        and I will ask that they not go
        but live longer to show the world
                their strength and beauty
        these Yucca blossoms
                adorned in splendor
                grasping upward
        moving ever higher
        towards the blazing sun—
                their fiery obliteration
        their final and most
        outrageous act.

Cold White Bone
(Persian Gulf "War")

The streets are quiet—
COLD WHITE BONE AND ALABASTER

The silence builds like a wall
creating a void
where questions drop like stones
and even wind makes little stir:
timid to the touch like a lover
who has been away, and can't
remember the
secret places of delight.

The morning light casts
its weak shadows of
ghostly buildings
sickly gray
under a hazy sky
of tattered rag blue

Seagulls gather
at the beach—
rise
screaming
at the sound of
human steps.

Sucked into murderous
acquiescence
we are moving to the broken drum

that raps skeletal fingers
of dirge
across
COLD WHITE BONE AND ALABASTER.

To G. C.

Gregory, if I may—
we never formally met
but smiled at one another
across a room, many years
ago
at one of Carolyn Del Gaudio's parties.

Yours was a pleasant smile
shy and fluttery as though afraid to settle
in the confines of your face.

Today I tripped quite by accident
across a street in North Beach
supposedly named innocuously
for Columbus.
Atop his dishonored name,
(as he discovered nothing
except a way to go down
in history)
was written CORSO.

CORSO means 'the road'
in Italian
and that is you
fellow poet-in-arms-
your life a series of early mishaps—
New York's child:
that city tried to do what it

would with you,
as Detroit to me.

But we were both stronger than that
Gregory
and emerged from all kinds
of prisons unscathed
except for the tips of our souls
which scorched
like
the wings of moths.

For Pablo Neruda

This day
like no other
will soon pass.

But now
the glamorous sea
flaunts her diamond surfaced brilliance.

The sun traverses the sky awakening other
worlds of sleepers

The moon will climb
its silken laddered perch
and embrace us in its
milky attraction
and a little sadness.

Soon, this day
like no other
will be gone.

Deep in the night
I feel the kiss of the sun
the murmured seduction of the
wind
the tingling feeling of sand on skin:

The results of this day unlike the morrow
or the morrow, or the morrow.

This day when we are alive.

Untitled

You think I am a woman alone,
and I have no rights?
Ha!
I spit out the fish-heads,
lamb's eyes
horse hooves
and pig's snouts.
I bite on the goat's tooth,
cow's eye
chicken's heart
and tiger's paw.

Better watch out!
I swear on my ancestors
better watch out!

You think I am a woman alone?!
the roar of my ancestors' war cries
is always with me,
the knowledge of my ancestors
lulls me to sleep each night!
Pig's snouts, horse's eye!
monkey feces
Ha!
Better watch out!
I'm gonna get you!

Rose petal nectar,
palm oil,
coconut kernel,
ju ju bead,
black eyed pea—
know what these mean?

Congo Square
smoke in the air.
Lion's heart
strange light in the dark.
Want my head?
I'll take yours instead!
Know gris gris?
It'll set you free.
Do unto others. . .
we're all sisters and brothers
Think I'm alone?
you must be stoned!!

We

I am a weed that refuses to go anywhere
unless I choose.

I am capricious and sour like bitteroot.

You are younger than the tenderest greens—
kind, hearty and enduring like the sun.

I am jaded, cynical and malformed—
my mind is an abyss.
I am bent, overworked, toughened by love,
afraid of love
lost in love.

You are ripe
optimistic
yearning
hopeful.
You are curious
naive
intelligent and strong like a young lion!

I am one.
We are two.

I am old enought to be your mother
tender enough to be your lover
afraid to be either

But. . .
this is not the perfect world
and because you are hungry

I am bread.

Katumwbe

Maketa, name from my father
Father, what is your name?
your lips are ripe like purple berries,
Your legs and arms are long and straight
like trees rising from the ground.
Your oblong head glistens, black

Father, what is your name?

you smile, father.
your eyes narrowing
your brow wrinkled
your head slightly inclined.

Father, we have lost the essence
you are named Levi, a jewish name
though your skin is ebony and velvet
as the night

Father, you are named Smith, an english name
though you speak with the tongues of african
wisdom

Father, what is your name?

I will name you love
and truth
and beauty

I will name you all that endures, like stone, and
wood
and animals of the night
and flowing rivers
and herbs of every kind
I will name you in all the tongues the spirits
have given
us to sing!
I will name you, as you named me Maketa, and
said,
"you do what you want with the last name!"

I have named us, Father.

Curbstone Press, Inc.
is a non-profit publishing house dedicated to literature that reflects a commitment to social change, with an emphasis on contemporary writing from Latin America and Latino communities in the United States. Curbstone presents writers who give voice to the unheard in a language that goes beyond denunciation to celebrate, honor and teach. Curbstone builds bridges between its writers and the public – from inner-city to rural areas, colleges to community centers, children to adults. Curbstone seeks out the highest aesthetic expression of the dedication to human rights and intercultural understanding: poetry, testimonials, novels, stories, photography.

This mission requires more than just producing books. It requires ensuring that as many people as possible know about these books and read them. To achieve this, a large portion of Curbstone's schedule is dedicated to arranging tours and programs for its authors, working with public school and university teachers to enrich curricula, reaching out to underserved audiences by donating books and conducting readings and community programs, and promoting discussion in the media. It is only through these combined efforts that literature can truly make a difference.

Curbstone Press, like all non-profit presses, depends on the support of individuals, foundations, and government agencies to bring you, the reader, works of literary merit and social significance which might not find a place in profit-driven publishing channels. Our sincere thanks to the many individuals who support this endeavor and to the following organizations, foundations and government agencies: ADCO Foundation, Witter Bynner Foundation for Poetry, Connecticut Commission on the Arts, Connecticut Arts Endowment Fund, Ford Foundation, Greater Hartford Arts Council, Junior League of Hartford, Lawson Valentine Foundation, LEF Foundation, Lila Wallace-Reader's Digest Fund, The Andrew W. Mellon Foundation, National Endowment for the Arts, Samuel Rubin Foundation and the Puffin Foundation.

Please support Curbstone's efforts to present the diverse voices and views that make our culture richer. Tax-deductible donations can be made by check or credit card to Curbstone Press, 321 Jackson St., Willimantic, CT 06226 Tel: (860) 423-5110.